JavaScript
For Babies

By Esmond Cooper

JavaScript helps us control websites.

Just like you have a remote to control your toy car, JavaScript lets you control things on a website by clicking and typing.

// Let's start our JavaScript adventure!

First, let's make the computer say "Hello, World!"
It's like saying "hi" to a new friend.

```
console.log("Hello, World!");
```

OUTPUT

Hello, World!

What if we want to make the computer ask our name?
We can use a question box!

```
var name = prompt("What is your name?");
```

OUTPUT

What is your name? |

If you type "Charlie," the computer puts "Charlie" into a box called "name."

We call these boxes "variables."

How can we make the computer say hello back?

```javascript
var name = prompt("What is your name?");
console.log("Hello, " + name + "!");
```

OUTPUT

What is your name? |

// If you type "Charlie":

Hello, Charlie!

Now, let's make the computer pick our favorite color.
We'll tell it our favorite is blue.

```
var favoriteColor = "blue";
console.log("My favorite color is " + favoriteColor + "!");
```

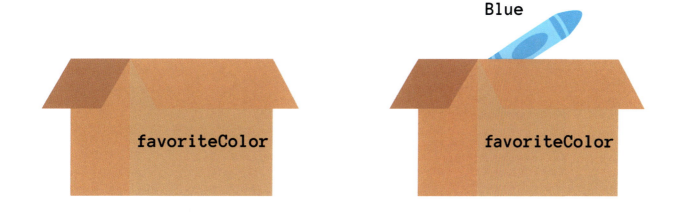

OUTPUT

My favorite color is blue!

Now, let's count to 3.
We tell the computer to count like we do with our fingers.

```
for (var number = 1; number <= 3; number++) {
  console.log(number);
}
```

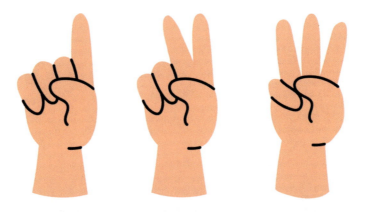

OUTPUT

1
2
3

Let's count backward from 3.

We'll tell the computer to start at 3 and go down.

```javascript
for (var number = 3; number > 0; number--)
{
  console.log(number);
}
```

OUTPUT

3

2

1

What if we want to say something many times?
Let's make it say "Yay!" three times.

```javascript
for (var i = 0; i < 3; i++) {
  console.log("Yay!");
}
```

OUTPUT

Yay!

Yay!

Yay!

Let's say "I love coding!" four times.

```javascript
for (var i = 0; i < 4; i++) {
  console.log("I love coding!");
}
```

OUTPUT

I love coding!

I love coding!

I love coding!

I love coding!

Can we make the computer do a funny dance?
Let's try with a loop!

```javascript
for (var i = 0; i < 3; i++) {
  console.log("Dance step " + step);
}
```

OUTPUT

Dance step 0

Dance step 1

Dance step 2

Dance step 3

Dance step 4

Can we play with numbers?

Yes! Let's add 2 and 3 together with JavaScript.

```javascript
var sum = 2 + 3;
console.log("2 + 3 is " + sum);
```

OUTPUT

2 + 3 is 5

If you have two apples and your friend gives you three more apples, now you have five apples. We call this adding things together.

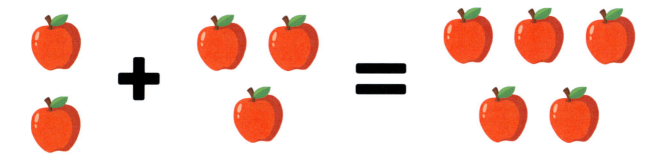

Let's subtract 2 from 3 with JavaScript.

```javascript
var sum = 3 - 2;
console.log("3 - 2 is " + sum);
```

OUTPUT

3 - 2 is 1

If you have three apples and you give two apples to your friend, now you only have one apple. We call this subtracting things.

Can the computer help us find a hidden toy?

Let's look for the teddy bear!

```
var toys = ["teddy bear", "train", "ball"];
console.log("I found the " + toys[0] + "!");
```

OUTPUT

I found the teddy bear!

Let's look for the train!

```
var toys = ["teddy bear", "train", "ball"];
console.log("I found the " + toys[1] + "!");
```

OUTPUT

I found the train!

Let's look for the ball!

```
var toys = ["teddy bear", "train", "ball"];
console.log("I found the " + toys[3] + "!");
```

OUTPUT

I found the ball!

What about making choices?
We can make the computer choose our snack. Apple or banana?

When var snack = "apple";

```js
var snack = "apple";
if (snack === "apple") {
  console.log("Yummy apple!");
} else {
  console.log("Tasty banana!");
}
```

OUTPUT

Yummy apple!

When var snack = "banana";

```js
var snack = "banana"";
if (snack === "apple") {
  console.log("Yummy apple!");
} else {
  console.log("Tasty banana!");
}
```

OUTPUT

Tasty banana!

You have a banana and an apple.

First, you need to put one of them into the "snack" box.

Let's put the apple in the box.

'IF' is like an apple scanner that can check if the box contains an apple or not.

If it's an apple, the apple 'IF' scanner says it's true.

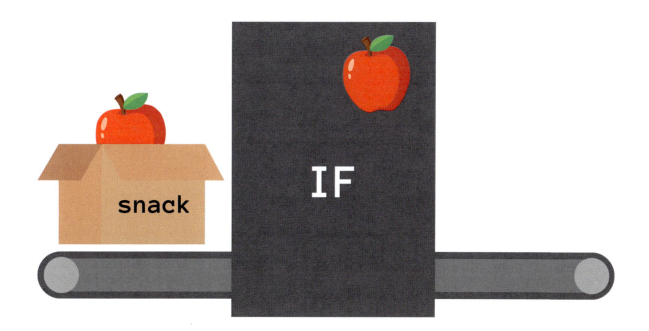

True

Now, let's put the banana in the box.

If it's a banana, the apple 'IF' scanner will say it's false.

False

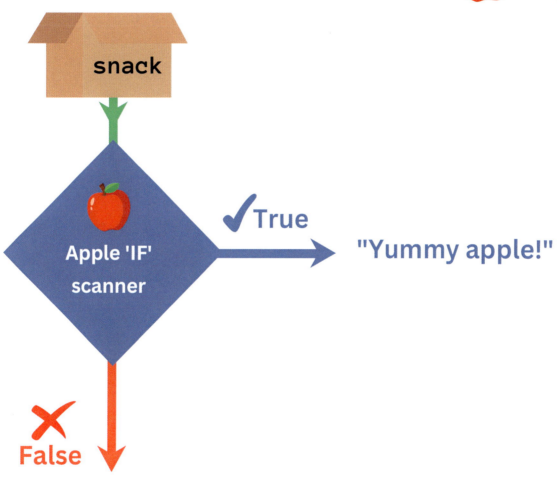

Let's use a banana 'IF' scanner.
What will the scanner say now?

Since it's a banana 'IF' scanner, it checks for bananas. Because the apple is not a banana, it shows 'false'.

False

Now, let's put the banana in the box.

Since it's a banana, the banana 'IF' scanner will say 'true'.

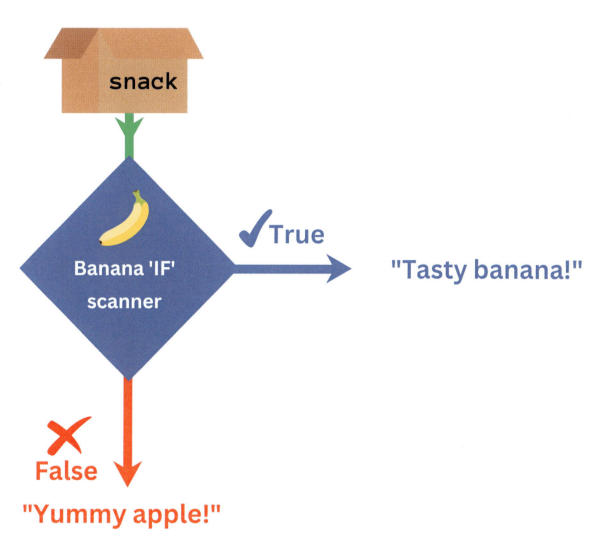

Let's play the number game: Is it big or small?
Let the computer decide!

When number = 5

```javascript
var number = 5;
if (number > 3) {
  console.log("Big number!");
} else {
  console.log("Small number!");
}
```

OUTPUT

Big number!

Let's play the number game: Is it big or small?
Let the computer decide!

When number = 1

```javascript
var number = 1;
if (number > 3) {
  console.log("Big number!");
} else {
  console.log("Small number!");
}
```

OUTPUT

Small number!

The computer checks if the number is greater than 3.

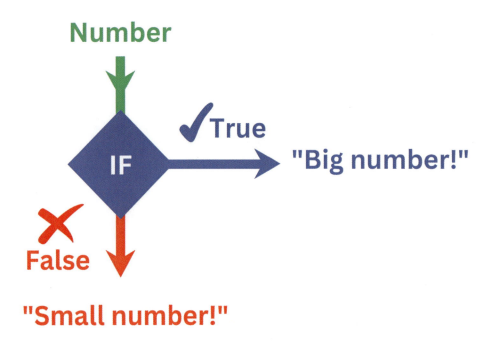

1. **The computer checks if the number (5) is greater than 3.**
2. **If it is, then the computer understands it's a "Big number!" and says so.**
3. **If the number was not bigger than 3, the computer would say "Small number!" instead.**

Is 4 bigger than 2? We can ask JavaScript.

```javascript
var number = 4;
if (number > 2) {
 console.log("Yes, 4 is bigger than 2!");
} else {
 console.log("No, 4 is not bigger than 2!");
}
```

OUTPUT

Yes, 4 is bigger than 2!

Manufactured by Amazon.ca
Bolton, ON